gulp\gasp

Serena Piccoli

Moria Books   Chicago   2022

Copyright © 2022

All rights reserved. No part of this book may be reproduced without the publisher's written permission, except for brief quotations in reviews.

Published by Moria Books.

All rights reserved.

ISBN: 979-8-9869421-0-0

First Edition

Moria Books
c/o Bill Allegrezza
9748 Redbud Rd. Munster, IN 46321

www.moriapoetry.com

Table of Contents

Acknowledgments	1
Preface by Adeena Karasick	3
gulp	
it's honey, darling!	10
I used to write love poems	11
the queen of herrings	14
greetings from summer 2022	15
and that	17
for rent	18
28th day	19
the sun kisses the prettiest	20
we call ourselves humans	
shingal	22
violet	23
liliana	24
the kingfisher in moria	26
bread and bandages	27
\liberté\égalité\fraternité\crimedesolidarité	28
capel celyn	30
the gold teeth	31
zanzibar island	
the woman of the hibiscus	34
jambiani moon	35
the wedding in the shamba	36
the well-organized chaos in stonetown	38
the obstinate monkeys	39
amore	
53rd day	41
dormant	42

your yarn	43
among ruins	44
at 3 am	46
the bluetit	47
foam	48
silvery rays	49
siren	50
murmuration	51

britannia

dissolution	53
the bore in arnside	54
the isle of man	56
as a white stone	57
manx morning choir	58
the cat	59
if	60

gasp

mary+raul = sex	62
where we are now	63
greetings from autumn 2020	64
the_pan_demic	66
english free school meals	67
eugeni and rostik	69
those 2 hands	70
we're the best\fuck the rest	71
gulp\gasp	72

Biography   74

Acknowledgements

This book contains poems written from spring 2019 to summer 2022, except for "Shingal," which was written in 2015, but as the indifference of the world to the slaughter of Kurds is still high, I want it in this book to raise awareness of their struggle. Apart from a couple of them written at the end of July 2022, the poems have been selected for publication in magazines and books worldwide, and for readings at Festivals.

I would like to thank all the publishers and directors of *Abridged, Giallo, the Sub-Saharan Magazine, the BeZine, Opiate Magazine, Tint Journal, Bridgewater International Poetry Festival, New Orleans Poetry Festival, Elba Poetry Festival, Concision Poetry, the Lit Quarterly Canada, Sonder Magazine, Prismatica, Ice Floe Press, 845 Press, Best Buds Collective, Tipping the Scales, Global Poemic, Floresta, Versante Ripido, Clay Literary, the Confessionalist, the Elpis Page, Coal Lick Run, the Dreaming Machine, Forever Endeavour, Letters with Wings, Wine Cellar Press, Vagabond Press, Poetry Health Service,* and *UK Places of Poetry.*

I thank William Allegrezza for publishing it after he published my chapbook *silviotrump* in 2017. I appreciate his work as a poet and a publisher, his political engagement through poetry, and the fact that everyone can download the PDF books of his publishing house for free from its website. Poetry can be a massive force to help people; therefore, it is important to have free access to books.

I thank Adeena Karasick for her preface and, above all, for her wonderful, loyal friendship.

I thank the Italian natural and urban landscape, along with its culture, that are always a source of inspiration and joy for me.

I thank the English and Manx natural and urban landscapes that have offered me inspiration, joy, and my second home.

I thank Alexandra, my fiancée, for the inspiration and the writing advice.

I thank poetry for making me the voice of the voiceless. Grazie!

Preface
Adeena Karasick

From the late 14th C., Flemish *gulpe* or Dutch *gulpen*, "gulp" is "to gush, pour forth, guzzle, swallow." Italian author, translator, and playwright, Serena Piccoli's stunning second English volume of poetry, *gushes forth* with an unstoppable flood of desire that is at once massively political and playful, negotiating contemporary local and global horrors, yet marked with an analytically observant, empathic regard for the interrelationship of lands, peoples, bodies, and animals, invoking a texturally complex sense of humanity, interrogating all that we thirstily "gulp down."

I personally have witnessed this sense of ardent engagement, in that as a world-class translator, Piccoli translated my virtually untranslatable spoken word opera, *Salomé: Woman of Valor / Salomé: donna di valore* from English into Italian, published by University of Padua Press, Italy in 2017, and together with her internationally produced poems, plays, and stunning photographs which like this volume of poetry are also grounded in feminist politics, further speaking to Piccoli's zealous commitment to cultural-political transformation and change. As a transplanted Italian now living in the British Isles, Piccoli has the unique vision of an outsider; a subaltern presence that not only gives voice to the voiceless as she gasps, grasps the ungraspable, speaks the unspeakable, and with passionate en[r]agement, journeys within a range of contested territories such as American colonization and warmongering, gender violence and homophobia, NATO, the Kurds, the English monarchy, antifascism, and intolerance.

Temporally composed between 2019-2022, punctuated with socio-political, cultural and linguistic shifts, and wry wordplay, *gulp\gasp* navigates the complexities within Italy, the British Isles, Zanzibar, and Europe, journalistically drawing on interviews, reports, photographs, essays and articles. For example, her playfully ironic list in

"#EnglishFreeSchoolMeals in January 2021," comprised of the actual menu the government provided to children in need: ("a bag for 10 days; / 2 jacket potatoes / 1 Heinz beans / 8 single cheese sandwiches / 2 carrots / 3 apples / 2 soreen / 2 bananas / 1 loaf of bread / 3 frubes / spare pasta / 1 tomato"). Or marked with a surrealistic sensibility, reflecting on the beauty and intimacy within this otherwise fraught era, points to ways, for example animals were regaining land. Take for instance, the astonishing image in "the_pan_demic," of 5 goats in a Welsh city center strolling down and doing some window shopping! Or in "for rent," "unfurnished apartment for rent / 1 bedroom mold and utilities included. . .no smoking – no pets - no poets / call Jack at lunch." Witty and keenly insightful, with a shoutout to John Ashbery's, *Lunch Poems, gulp\gasp* provides us with a defamiliarizing charm, leaving us thirsting for more.

According to Piccoli, "[*Gulp*] aims to stimulate debate about the state of our society. I wish to raise awareness." And *so it does*, reminding us of Blair and Bush invading Iraq and their lies and their bombs, and it lives uncomfortably with how Tony Blair was knighted in June, when Priti Patel, the Minister of Defence, signed the extradition of Julian Assange to the USA. Riddled with frustration and satirical energy, each poem offers a raw glimpse into Piccoli's worldview assessing crimes against humanity, oppression, transgression, injustice: "We're the best\fuck the rest," "greetings from autumn 2020," "greetings from summer 2022," "the gold teeth," "I used to write love poems," all depict her vehement grievances towards NATO; how there are 120 NATO military bases in Italy, from where Americans bombed Serbia, Iraq, Syria. She is writing against the lies, the social injustice the US has inflicted on Europeans, against the high expenditure of arms by the BoJo government, the long imprisonment and extradition of Julian Assange (US and UK again), the supposed cultural supremacy of the West and its racism, hate, neocolonialism, exploitation, social injustices, and exported democracies. Governments that have worshipped zerocovid policy when a massive number of important studies showed that zerocovid policy doesn't make any sense at all, stating, "it's just - once again – oppression." African migrants criminalized for escaping wars, violence, famine, the diminutization of women. Serena Piccoli is "sick of all this," and *gulp\gasp* provides a litanic map through these varied territories of inequity:

> sitting at their luxury table of lies and nails
> their capitalist jaws laughing at us
>
> 4 incisors of exporting democracy
> 4 canines of oppression
> 4 incisors of brainwashing
> 4 molars of slavery
>
> the prolonged grinding and grating of
>
> 4 premolars of hypocrisy
> 4 molars of stolen land
> 4 premolars of stereotypes
> 4 molars of injustice

And sometimes, these poems are marked by a keen sense of irony: whether it be in "the queen of herrings," ideologically questioning the monarchy, and the stark socio-economic disparities in the UK revisited in "Greetings from Summer 2022:" "they're feasting / while we're fasting / we'll eat the rich / while we're watching the fish," or the painful irony of being misgendered in Zanzibar in the autobiographical, "the wedding in the shamba," where Piccoli recounts how while teaching pedagogy in the African village they believed her to be a man, and the abuse and discrimination of gender disparity in traditional Zanzibar[bar]ic culture, or the profound paradox of contemporary democracy, whose antifascist left-wing policies have led to violence and repression (the so called "fascism of the antifascists").

Though formally witty, playful and punningly provocative, each piece packs a hard punch; and as such, serves as a powerful tool for raising awareness. Take, for example, *gulp\gasp's* vivid depictions regarding the plight of the Kurds, in "shingal," "bread and bandages," "those 2 hands," recounting the "2014 systematic rape of 3 thousand Yazidi Kurdish Women"— sentiments shared in her award-winning plays, or highlighting the persistence of modern slavery in the south of Italy, where according to Piccoli, "migrants from both Africa and eastern Europe live in shacks, work 12 hours under the flaming sun, picking tomatoes, many of them victims of sexual and physical violence." And through pounding insistence, she exposes their wrenched plight:

> the sun kisses the prettiest.
> It's an Italian saying
> he says
> 3 euros per hour\12 hours per day
> the red gold burning in his ears
> between the toes\up the ass
> picking tomatoes 7 days a week
> bent and burnt
> crashing in the shack with a stroke
> the red mud boss' boots
> pushed him down the creek at noon
> before stripping…
> the sun kisses the prettiest.
> Lucky you
> he said

And as [the page rages], continuing to voice the voiceless, "the kingfisher in Moria" presents Moria, an abhorrent migrant camp in the Mediterranean, riddled with very poor health conditions, invisible to the beachgoing public. Exquisitely exposing the contrast of the sultry, placid Mediterranean juxtaposed against the horror of Moria, *gulp\gasp* sings "their song of despair // carried on electric blue feathers from / their shacks built with dust and revenge;" sentiments extended in "liberté/ egalité/fraternité/crime de solidarité" where through waves of sonic repetition, speaks to ways it was a crime ("of solidarity") to help migrants passing through France or entering France, yet provides some well needed hope: where "snow . . . the light in the darkness of our march."

But though grounded in robust politics, this must-read collection is also marked by great love. And even though she ironically opens with how "I *used* to write love poems," *gulp/gasp* gushes with passionate longing and connectedness. For example, in "53rd day" dedicated to her lover, Alexandra, written during the 6 interminable months of early Covid, Spring 2020, when they had to live across the continent from each other, beckons her lover from abroad,

> and as you're combing your hair
> craving my hands…
> lie in bed and make love with
> my smell…hear my
> arms singing
> with the Nightingales.

This sense of wistful yearning is further manifested with an amorous regard for nature, wildlife, and ecosystems which mirror bodies and behaviors. With a profound ecopoetic sensibility, the poems are populated with starlings, bluetits, bees, deer, ferns, wildflowers, pheasants, seagulls, where "sheep seals geese twined and twisted in sky's harmony." And, like how for Piccoli, "the muezzin squeaks in stereophony," so it is that *gulp\gasp* provides us with a love that is polyphonic, multiple, and fluid, combining a range of identities and foci.

The cover of the book is a photo by Piccoli (who is also a renowned photographer), depicting a wall of graffiti, tagged, "NONSENSE." The white typography is locked within a blood red block inscribed on a white-washed decomposing brick wall. The image is striking in that not only does it speak to the scarlet darknesses and discriminations that *gulp\gasp* grapples with, but highlights at the outset, that "nonsense" is *not* "no sense" but navigates through a polyglossic heterogeneity of angles, codes, discourses, opinions, and through the endless barrage of information / disinformation, we must continually unpack "the sense" between all that which is illogical, irrational, relational, in an incendiary supra-sensorious nascence of contradiction and paradox.

    Fittingly, the book opens with a poem about human stupidity – "it's honey, darling!" and ends on the title poem, "gulp\gasp," recounting all the lies, the violence, the social injustices, the hate we've gulped down yet states, "still I hear the gasp of the calm." This final line, which stands alone surrounded by open space, reads as the gasp of all of us, the enshrouded vagrants, migrants, and misrepresented. And through gasps, rasps, maps, as we gasp the un-gaspable, grasp the ungraspable, this gripping volume asks one to not "sow silence" but to think strategically about *what* and *how* we are gulping in our ever-unquenchable thirst for knowledge, eros, truth, and meaning.

gulp

it's honey, darling!

we've killed all the Bees

now – as we're the smartest on earth
at the same time once a month
we all stand outside tongue out
to lick one drop of acid rain

and imagine it's honey

I used to write love poems

I used to write love poems
to flowers/birds/my fiancée

but their grinding teeth have been too loud

sitting at their luxury table of lies and nails
their capitalist jaws laughing at us

4 incisors of exporting democracy
4 canines of oppression
4 incisors of brainwashing
4 molars of slavery

the prolonged grinding and grating of

4 premolars of hypocrisy
4 molars of stolen land
4 premolars of stereotypes
4 molars of injustice

I used to write love poems
but their grinding teeth
have been screaming and imposing orders
all our lives

with their

receding gums of hunger/malnutrition/poverty
cavities of police brutality
a crown of classism
a tongue for propaganda as their lingua franca

grinding, gritting with their

palate for coups

roots of state racism
the bad breath of disablism
saliva of male chauvinism

And no
no wisdom teeth at all

But
I have a tongue too and a voice and hands that write

I'm not your subject
I'm not your little fish
Keep your bloody teeth off my land/life/love/body

I don't want a white father state
I don't want your decrepit views on how I must lead my life
I don't want your classist racist misogynist colonialist white
suprematist liberticidal oppression

I don't wanna help you preserve the billionaire class buffet
or those in power who consume us to starvation

Julian showed us the diamonds decorating your table
saying

quieta non movere et mota quietare
don't move things that are at rest, and put at rest things that
move

I still write love poems
and I also move

non ducor, duco
I am not led, I lead my life

I'll never rest under your bloody bite
of torture and impunity

and your spit
of fake erosive rule

the queen of herrings

the queen of herrings froze her subjects with her speech
her 2billionBrooch dropped exhausted

the prime herring invited them
to sacrifice for herring immunity

they all died

cod save the queen

greetings from summer 2022

at 6 am every day I drive down to Marciana Marina
to watch 10 different species of fish
watching my goofy swimming

Elba Island and its blooming bougainvillaea
Roman ruins overlooking the azure sea
an old piazza and a little church perched on mountains

Beauty makes us resist

1000 miles from here
Tony Blair is being made a knight
his co-invasion of Iraq in 2003 ushered hundreds of thousands
into death and chaos

The constant fear
is the spring behind their
lawmaking\warmaking

B&B cast Saddam as a global threat
who possessed weapons of mass destruction
After 19 years has anyone found such weapons?

The constant fear
to oppress us all
imposed by the propaganda
of masters and arse-lickers

The fish in front of me are whistling and wondering
what the hell I'm thinking

Tony Blair's becoming knight in Windsor Castle
a few miles away from Belmarsh prison
where Julian Assange has been ill for years
and stuck in arbitrary imprisonment

unconvicted
for political reasons
for revealing B&B's crimes

Anger makes us speak up

us and them
they're feasting
while we're fasting

we'll eat the rich
while we're watching fish

we'll eat the capitalist prophet
while he's dying to make profit

they're fishing for our data
we'll feed them with fatal feta

they'll be starving
they're not used to it

while bingeing on a fake buffet
choking on pork stew

they'll tell us to obey again
but many will refuse

they'll tell us to trust their mandate
but - gutted and disgusted - we'll deconstruct it

The blue bay is too beautiful
to be missed - again - for their oppression
--
Beauty makes us survive

and you think fish are useless

and that

in a brownbricked semidetached house
in winding SpringRoad, Wrecsam
in a snaking row of brownish hours
a man staggered a pumpkin
in a damp kitchen

and then
bricked silence continued

it was too orange\too round\too calm for him

and that
was just the beginning of Autumn

for rent

unfurnished apartment for rent
1 bedroom - mold and utilities included
overlooking the moat and the mouse
no smoking - no pets - no poets
call Jack at lunchtime
—
enjoy your lunch, Jack
all poets are dead

28th day

    while Nature keeps going
      we hold our breath
        still and torn
     among tulips erect

and in the lurking vastness that crushes us
he's sieving the soil to find his mother's ashes

the sun kisses the prettiest

the sun kisses the prettiest.
It's an Italian saying
he says

3 euros per hour\12 hours per day
the red gold burning in his ears
between the toes\up the ass

picking tomatoes 7 days a week
bent and burnt
crashing in the shack with a stroke

the red mud boss' boots
pushed him down the creek at noon
before stripping his poor pendant

the sun kisses the prettiest.
Lucky you
he said

we call ourselves
humans

shingal

to Kurdish women fighting Daesh

August 3rd 2014
systematic rape of 3thousand Yazidi Kurdish Women

on the liquor stores they destroy
they spray the name of the caliph
with drug and booze in the pockets

we're all running to Mount Shingal
no water\food\shelter from the west
up here the only plant is tiny
like mercy

some humans are more humans than others
some women are less people than others

I left Germany to go back to my homeland
we all live for our dead women
take up arms\philosophy\politics

you don't protect us - we self\defend EachOther
until yesterday I had to stay home waiting to be married
waiting for western help
I laid out my braid on her and said:
I'll come, I'll see, I'll conquer

I leave you the rose from that tiny plant on Shingal
a Rose has thorns not to attack
but to defend

violet

to Mojgan Kavoosi,
Kurdish writer arrested in Iran

rushing\working\clicking
we're too busy to notice
the purple\yellow violet
sprouting from cement
in our spring

compulsive saving
bingeing on telly
over here

while over there
she sees and speaks
about mass protests
against petrol prices

cos *silence is treason*
she says
and gets sentenced to
76 months

though far away from that spring
I'm busy thinking
of the purple\yellow violet
sprouting from jail cement

loudly tossing its head
in our defense

liliana

to Liliana Segre

I am the grandmother of that little girl
who was expelled at the age of 8 from school
we're Jews - dad said.

I have a name now and am still Jewish

I am the grandmother of that little girl
hairless skeleton in Auschwitz
no colour\time\senses

The dog was watching, the guard was beating up bones
some bread in the excrement was her lunch
the girl with no breasts\age\period\underpants

I have a name now, my identity

The girl was digging holes for water pipes
every hour every day
but no time existed, only bones, smoke and ashes

When she picked up a dried apricot out of the camp
she tasted freedom again
and started repeating
memory keeps democracy healthy

I am the grandmother of that little girl who gives me no peace
because it is war – always
because fascism never died and can kill in the most innocent
guise

I am the mother of all of you who keep fighting
and will fight
the abomination that I've survived

I am Liliana, still with that number on my arm
I will die as I have lived
with history on my skin

the kingfisher in moria

to those in Moria camp

the orange breasted bird
flew past my shoulders and sang
behind my back
their song of despair

carried on electric blue feathers
from their shacks
built with dust and revenge
topped with sparks of metal

the orange breasted bird was flying there
above the filthy ruins of former humanity
in a dance of love
to courtship its soul mate

in a day that evens joy and torment

bread and bandages
to Kurdish people

let's go beyond
disseminating info/facebook photos

send school buses\help new businesses
send baking equipment/run English classes

no bread left in Afrin country
no Left left in fascist country

raise voices/raise funds
time to be aware
women fighters die from blood loss
waiting for care

it's not a possibility
it's a necessity

let's send hemostatic dressings
let's go make bread and bandages

to stop bleeding from
fascism
patriarchy
capitalism

let's go beyond all
let's go to Rojava and Shingal!

/liberté/egalité/fraternité/crimedesolidarité/

liberté
I'm Destinity, my baby's been in me for 7 months
so has cancer. I've lost my job in Italy
now I know the word snow
I limp on mountains
to France:
to my sister's.
///
égalité
children are all the same
have had the third in me for 8 months
marching
Omar's in my husband's arms on Alps:
I don't want my kids mining cobalt
for whites' smartphones.
///
skilift/skipass/
trekking/rafting/
NO TRESPASSING/
///
fraternité
In the white quicksand
limping
hardly breathing
godhelpme
heavy belly
exhausted
chill running in me
godhelpme
he carries me
we're all in the fast car
white on the White everywhere
in me
makes me sick
godhelpme

SnowMan, as my husband calls him
stops the car
in the middle of the white nowhere
shouting/getting off
writhed on white and kids'cries
he shouts *hopital* and others shout.

No. We have no papers
Godhelpme

crime de solidarité
Benoit/SnowMan is halted by police
and by 5 possible years in prison
my third son is in my arms
we'll be quickly sent back home
I only want my baby Benoit not end up mining.
/ / /
the snow is the light in the darkness of our march
this White world makes me sick
they stop us in France
abandon in Italy
3 a.m. the railway station's closed
I my husband my baby in me
no help outside
the day will come
and someone will.

The light on glasses nearly appears
while I'm disappearing for you.

capel celyn

to the last inhabitants of Capel Celyn, Wales

the day we sold the last cow we remembered
none of us had ever stolen one
standing in a spiral around the cattle
hats and coats\boots and belts
all 70 of us tight knit together

one summer day
thirsty artificial humans out of nowhere
came to force us to leave
our 12 houses\school\buried relatives
under water

we went marching to town hall
the 80 year old lady with 3 year old Eurgain
to protest the theft

they were spitting\throwing tomatoes
at us

then they installed an english only signpost
facing our chapel
construction of the Tryweryn reservoir

and I – with love and anger and cow blood - wrote
why not drown Liverpool?

the gold teeth

sat down to write a poem
about UK and £16bn\military\spending\spree
that'll increase the existing £41bn\budget

higher than ever
since the cold war

they must know UFOs are about to attack

went googling articles to read and be accurate
but couldn't read any, apart from:

*Register for free and continue reading
Answer the question below to reveal the rest of the article:
how often does your dog get an oral care regime?*

finally, a tycoon-haunted newspaper article
*I have done this in the teeth of the pandemic, amid every other
demand on our resources, because the defence of the realm and the
safety of the British people must come first.*

A girl suffers from a common chronic disease and gp says
the nhs cannot pay for her vital medicines

so she must pay 300 pounds a box

*if there was one policy which strengthens the UK in every possible
sense, it is building more ships for the royal navy*

she also pays 300 pounds for an ecg

but the Teeth\the Realm\the Bribes\the Navy
come before your health

no wonder

we need to cure a dog's teeth
to access news to read

zanzibar island

the woman of the hibiscus

to Giorgia

I sleep
in a hut of palms
with you and the restless woodworm

as the sun comes up
with the elegance of the hibiscus
you leave on a pilgrimage of wishes

I watch over
dry banana trees and wannabe mangoes
and I lose to cards with Monkeys

When in the afternoon all stops
nothing stops:
orange\green veils along the road
sell baobab fruits
(that I don't buy, cos you don't like them)
the saucepan on the ground steams cinnamon fumes
and tree roots pop out of the lagoon

the first Mangrove Moon leaves the boats on the shore
and brings you back home
with an empty booty
and melancholy in your pocket.

I sleep
in the echo of Monkeys laughing
with you and your restless brainworm

jambiani moon

the barefoot southern cross
winds thru sleeping mangoes
while the moon reclaims its waters
of women and shores

the silence of rustling palms
spurs the wary heron
to fish and bath
as she summons all

the dark bright night
swings and springs
among those walking miles
and resting on hot cement

the barefoot southern cross
admits the regality of the moon
as she grants gifts
to toothless sailors

the wedding in the shamba

in the forest of white trunks
we pass thru sweats of dust
and violet banana trees

they're waiting for us at the wedding
to have lunch on the ground among skinny hens
and have rice with our hands

the muezzin squeaks in stereophony
and whining singsongs make women dance in circle
as men - ferocious and bored
on the edge of the wall
are looking at them

we get in the mother's shanty
we're Wazungu, white women
guests of the village of colorful veils

the only small floor
overflows with girls

gracious – they open the door
fat – sleep on the ground
sweaty – their boobs hit me
shy – think I'm a boy

you choke, right before seeing the bride
and thoughts of dust sweat even more

in a small room falling in
crammed with mosquito nets\breaths\dampness\
a mannequin of a doll been sitting for hours
tied
with rented heavy golden chains

the bride is a mental catafalque

eyes wide open under a closed veil
in thick black makeup
swollen feet in heavy heels

as you faint
thinking that you might have been tied to that fate
the husband
stiff and solemn in his white costume and the scimitar
makes his way thru the crowd with a fake body guard.

And I
who'd wish to lie under the banana flowers
I can hear in the wind
gay Monkeys gargling

the well-organised chaos of stonetown

caged chicken on roads
deflated ox cart
seller of empty tanks only

280 flies on 199 rice beans
clothes hang in the fishy smell
seller of carrots only

tamarind icipops\hot corn
exchange of cinnamon and flip flops
seller of potatoes only

And on the pavement that roars with sweat
the Tailor sitting at his Singer
sows Silence

the obstinate monkeys

the chant of the waiting keeps echoing
empty – in the thick jungle
just me and an offended Monkey

I swim white under blue fruit
the most stupid one is me and she knows it.
Sometimes we eat leaves and spit autumn
then she scatters pomegranate from my hand

At night we look at each other
Me, Monkey, Moon
til the first gets crossed eyed
and the second sits and bides

Every now and then we remember the Woman of Silences:
Moon says that she'd play the flute for her
Monkey insists on saying that she couldn't hear
(behind red plants I'm dreaming like Rousseau)
The other monkey insists on saying
I can hear her, and see her!

oh, ash hush, sweet charm
she'll love you till she flies

the Monkey is rite: the most stupid one is me

amore

to Alexandra

53rd day

fickle walls
fragment my body
in this no-time\no-space\shit

no page books
and 12 broken clocks
trap me in

the steady loud drill
and a quirky roof
12 inches above me

no petal daisies in the bin
mold on a dead mannequin
and in between

the sudden breath
of your shimmering verse

dormant

the door is ajar
I shut it
to let you finally sleep

while I   behind it
am swinging along
with your dormant stag

your yarn

once my arms were buried in red sand
one leg was hung on an elder, one on an alder

then you appeared in the distance
walking with placid sheep

silently sat and span
sewed my pieces in the heath

and wove you
into me

among ruins

to lgbtq immigrants

we 2 stand tall among ruins

I don't look around anymore like when I was alone
now I only have time to get into your
eyes\belly\breast\mouth\vagina\arms
and I do not see the burning dust

I remember the runaways that feel illegal in your country
those who don't know where to start
because they've never talked about\to themselves
those who had sex in a hurry\instinctively
those who tell lies because they've been surviving in this way
those who drown in the water of the mirage

the bricks roll to the ground to the sound of
"*don't be an homosexual because you offend god*"
if god is offended, then it offends me
or maybe I don't care

the dust rises and falls on "*you're too feminine to be a lesbian*"
thud of stones and sky "*homosexuality is a Western perversion*"
another high collapse "*homosexuality is a modern fashion*"

and while you landed inside me
fleeing from corrective rape -
because lesbians - and on top of that black - should be
straightened up
the ruins
were demonstrating hatred in the city of youthful love

and now, my Love,
while I hold you with my eyes
and I suck you with my hands

I'm more powerful than any collapse in law that can take you
away

while on these stones
we bloom in paper

at 3 am

on a night far away from yours
I'm under an ancient chestnut tree
pink feathers are mirrored on the sunset river
and the slow flow is bathing the Flamingo

At this time you're combing your hair
craving my hands
putting some Moon and makeup on
to lie in bed and make love with my smell

in the windy darkness
the eyes of love and the smiles of joy
brighten up trees and shores

and while you're dreaming of us and can't fall asleep
I finally hear my arms singing
with the Nightingales

the bluetit

on a silent fig tree
a Bluetit stands proud
black make-up around her eyes
overlooking the waste land

she looks fragile\she's not
still trilling in the ill wind

all the leaves have gone
the waterfall still frozen

her yellow belly holds a wish:
hopes the dawn is in love with her
as she sings to it

the dawn rises every day
for its love for the Bluetit

foam

66 sheep in line in a frosty field
2 grouse shelter in a hole in the snow
while slow amber falls on deer

2 close-knit ravens are not killing now

breathing the foam of the slow
low tide

all is still

but my muscles unwinding
in your warm foam

silvery rays

nobody sees me
I don't exist

        You're whirling on winding waves
           shaping silvery tides
         in the pearly pacing foam

you see me
and make me come

           sculpting wandering waves
             into a round shell
          lifted back into silvery rays

siren

they started whirling the rumor I was a monster
swimming around me till I drank it
as it washed away the sea flowers in me
I became the monster

couldn't lye on the rock among the others
nor in the silvery foam
anticipation drowned:
you wouldn't get to me
trapped in the flowing storms of voices

I was the monster
I would scare you

the high tide again
brought another shipwreck

and out of the blue
sinewy arms gently swimming
rushed to reach my forgotten flowers

your bronze caring creature
met my eyes and hopes
while my hair was swinging with the waves

when you first held me
I killed the monster

and saved myself
for us

murmuration

the hypnotising flock of starlings
swoop and swirl in shifting shapes

silencing your sleep
contracting and expanding
fear and dream

they shift air in a virtuoso wind
murmuring through your breath

now the coral pink petal
is falling on your hair
like the kiss from my hand

britannia

dissolution

strongly binding together
      sixteen of us
         sound and supportive

          strong marks on bricks under
       stone vaults

sitting in a circle overlooking the
sea, we heal you with herbs
     sail a ferry to the promised land

          spiral staircases keep us safe
      so do uneven stairs

     see? nothing here is accidentally made

the bore in arnside

on top of the hill the wood never sleeps
and the lady is heating milk
for 7-year Addison
meditating over bees

he remembers that in 1666 England was under a heat wave

on top of the hill I graze and gaze the high sea tide
flowing towards the river
meeting in the bore

Different waters mingle together

a young deer is running towards me
thru fern and wildflowers
it stops – nose to nose

Different eyes mingle together

I can hear the waves approaching
bowing holding
pausing

it turns right and rushes into the wood

the wave hug is released

on top of the hill
the raven has a worm in his beak
bees are still working hard
and a fly stings my arm

I hear
the old breeze caressing the lake
a worm falling off a flying raven

and the music Addison's offering us
by random pressing the piano keys

different waters mingle together

the isle of man

nothing is harsh here
not even the Pheasant call

as a white stone

the wind is painting the field
golden blue with purple bells
tossing their heads
thru barley stretching
under flocks of geese

wind turns a dark green cliff
into a patchwork of shades
snaking around
ancient cottages and little stone bridges

a white dot
over a cobalt sea:
a parading seagull alone
as impudent as a white stone

manx morning choir

to Pippa and Su

a single interlacing of voices
sheep, seals, geese
twined and twisted
in sky harmony

the overs and unders
fly on different tunes
horizontal and vertical
dawn to noon

the musical patterns
lavishly repeated
in form and similarity
reverse from noon to sunset

these ancient wool, books and stones
are twined and twisted
in the illusory nature
of Celtic knots

while all these vivid windy colours
on cliffs and fields
prove the verity
of Nature's knots

the cat

every monastery has a cat
to protect food and minds

we're hunting words
it's hunting mice

we store corn and read a chapter
through high tides and strong winds

and as we shelter travellers
in our vaulted peace

the Cat foresees its solitude
in the smell of the glen

if

nibbled mouldy almonds
decomposing plums of undefinable colour
the unknown dead spider
on an orange that left Africa 3 months ago
hard persimmons for playing bowling
and the solitude of the putrefied lemon in the microwave

if the apocalypse comes
nothing will change for us

gasp

mari+raul = sex

we were cancelling cartoons\scenes\words
then lives
*Australian police arrest quarantine escapees\the teenage trio fled a
remote 14day detention camp by scaling a fence at night*

we blame & find new scapegoats
rule and divide\worship zerocovid

after years of waiting in vain
democracy supporters can now suppress millions of people
quietly
unseen
we want you! to cancel you

we've created the perfect enemy\ to treat like dictators do
this is our long-awaited moment\let us hate you and beat you
and imprison you and mock you

a lone wandering kid writes his joy on parliament wall
Mari+Raul=Sex

the newspapers show how beer gardens can boost our sex drive
and remind it's your turn to wear the scarlet letter

while the Ghost of the Flea
is wandering around
this delirium
in the armamentarium
of the momentum

where we are now

to Breonna Taylor

the hideous statue has finally fallen\
\
dust on too many ashes\

greetings from autumn 2020

2 prominent Italians are returning their legion of dis honour awards
- France's highest -
in protest at president Macron's decision to give the award to his
friend the Egyptian president al-Sisi

        a good friend closes his eyes to
        kidnapping\torture\killing
        of
        students\researchers\protesters
        and other human rights violations

the 2 Italians accuse al-Sisi of being
        objectively complicit
        as head of state
        in the criminal behaviour committed by his men

I turn the page and the rage.
Think of Giulio Regeni
and read on

an assistant professor in US has been called by colleagues
        miss missy
        honey hon
        sugar pumpkin
        cutie darling
        girl ma'am
        student secretary
        sweetheart sweetie

I turn the rage

UK pm Johnson is increasing Britain's investment in defence to
its highest level
since the Cold War
        this is our chance to end the era of retreat

transform our armed forces
bolster our global influence
defend our people
and way of life

a woman in her late 20s suffering from severe ME\chronic fatigue
has lost her benefits while looking for a flat to share with her fiancée in England
1 year quest and no penny from the state
her fiancée has lost her job – due to management of the pandemic
can't find one
and of course no penny from the state that imposed the lockdowns

the young woman keeps being rejected

we don't accept tenants on benefits
only professionals are accepted by the mortgage company

and the lit mag is asking me to write a poem
about my hopes for the new year

the_pan_demic

she used to eat at restaurants
table for one
now she's forced at home
practising the basics
of bacon for breakfast

in the opposite quarantined house
they're having spinach and monoliths for supper
as the queen of herrings
explains why you can't make an omelette
without breaking any eggs

and as everyone strives and despairs
and the bacon is not sizzling
cos the pan is demic,
5 mountain goats on main road
are happily regaining what's theirs

#EnglishFreeSchoolMeals in January 2021

a bag for 10 days:

2 jacket potatoes

1 Heinz beans
(Beans, Tomatoes, Water, Modified Cornflour, Spirit Vinegar, Salt, Natural Flavouring, Spice Extracts, Sweetener - Steviol Glycosides, Herb Extract)

8 single cheese sandwiches

2 carrots
3 apples

2 soreen
(Fortified Wheat Flour, Raisins, Partially Inverted Sugar Syrup, Colour: E150c, Barley Malt Extract, Maize Starch, Rice Starch, Vegetable Fat (Rapeseed, Palm), Salt, Preservative)

2 bananas
1 loaf of bread

3 frubes
(Yogurt, Skimmed Milk Powder, Lactic Cultures, Sugar 7.1%, Modified Manioc and Maize Starch)

spare pasta
1 tomato
—
your children will either starve
or die of a diet related disease
---
the bag is issued instead of £30 vouchers
the bag of capitalism

---
this is not poetry
this is poverty

eugeni and rostik

to Svetlana

Eugeni has just turned 18
he wears Ronaldo's fake jersey
sent by his mum Svetlana
a carer in Italy

she lives with Carolina - 101 year old
who every afternoon repeats
I am the way into the city of woe
I am the way into eternal pain
I am the way to go among the lost

Eugeni doesn't want, bus soon he'll have to

he's stuck at home with Rostik, his 13 year old bro
among Chechen militias and low flying Russian planes

after so many years he cries out for mum

she's stuck in Italy
can't send money or food
no safe buses to Ukraine

he'll soon have to go and fight

Rostik looks at burning fields
he should cross them
freedom is in Poland

granny keeps praying the christian god
with no benefits
Eugeni can't focus on anything
he's only made a decision:
he'll go
with Ronaldo's jersey

those 2 hands

*to the Kurds facing extradition
from Sweden and Finland*

once upon a time a basket seller
entertained his waiting clients with a folktale:

2 hands of 2 different bodies
were considered respected\peaceful

jewels were worn on those fine pale fingers
who wrote different languages

one day the 2 shook hands with the Ghost of the Fleas
they moved and bowed to show approval of his acts

all fleas were inhabited by the shadows of bloodthirsty men
the Ghost always held a cup for blood drinking

a penumbra wandering and killing
needed to suppress shadows to expand his powers

one day the 2 hands signed the long memorandum
of his ghastly demands

they were ready to give up the shadows of their own people
for the Ghost to have them drown in muddy waters

but the 2 hands, the fleas and the Ghost didn't know
that the only thing that never drowns is a shadow

we're the best\fuck the rest

we're the civilized
we kill civilians for their own sake
we own democracy
we'll sell it to you at a high price

you spread propaganda\we spread information
we rule and divide you
if we say you lie then it's true
if you say we lie then it's fake

whoever is near you - dead or alive - is our enemy
a baker who serves you bread must be killed

surrender to our explosive democracy
we're charming\with bright teeth
we've created you\you're now our enemy

but - hey - we warned you, buddy
we shape democracy\with our steel teeth

gulp\gasp

                                all the erupting noise
                              is gulped down the beak

        and I hear

the seashell falling on cement

                                      ravens are smart
                            they kill and cause no pain
                              for a guilt-free meal

        still I hear

                                    the gasp of the clam

Serena Piccoli is an Italian poet, playwright, photographer, and artistic director. She writes both in Italian and English about contemporary political and social issues with a touch of irony. Her previous chapbook, *silviotrump*, was published by Locofo Chaps (USA).

Her poems and plays are featured in anthologies and magazines in the UK, USA, Canada, Australia, Ireland, Nigeria, Italy and Romania. Her plays have been successfully staged throughout Italy. She is invited to festivals all over the world. Her photographs have been featured in magazines and art galleries all over the world.

She is the co-founder and artistic director of the International Poetry and Sister Arts Festival in Cesena (Italy) along with Giorgia Monti.

She holds a column of Italian contemporary poetry in the historical and most prominent cultural magazine in Romania, *Tribuna*. She is the co-founder (with Giorgia Monti) of the Association Lestordite which aims to spread poetry (Italy).

She is the Italian translator of poet and professor Adeena Karasick along with Pina Piccolo. She has also translated African women poets into Italian.

She is the co-founder of La Betonica Theatre Company (Padova, Italy) along with Alberto Moni.

She enjoys writing collaborative poems with William Allegrezza.

She holds two bachelor degrees (one as an interpreter and translator, Padova, Italy; one in Performing arts, top grade *cum laude*, Ferrara, Italy) and one master degree in Theatre and Performing Arts, top grade, IUAV University of Venice.

She loves nature, friendship, the sea and all the arts. She enjoys good food, wine, chocolate, summer, cycling, swimming and travelling. She can't stand social injustice.
www.serenapiccoli.com

Books/E-Books Available from Moria Books

Jordan Stempleman's *Their Fields* (2005)
Donna Kuhn's *Not Having an Idea* (2005)
Eileen R. Tabios's *Post Bling Bling* (2005)
Anny Ballardini's *Opening and Closing Numbers* (2005)
    Garin Cycholl's *Nightbirds* (2006)
lars palm's *Mindfulness* (2006)
Mark Young's from *Series Magritte* (2006)
Francis Raven's *Cooking with Organizational Structures* (2006)
Raymond Bianchi's *American Master* (2006)
Clayton Couch's *Letters of Resignation* (2006)
Thomas Fink's *No Appointment Necessary* (2006)
Catherine Daly's *Paper Craft (2006)*
Amy Trussell's *Meteorite* Dealers (2007)
Charles A. Perrone's *Six Seven* (2008)
Charles Freeland's *Furiant, Not Polka* (2008)
Mark Young's *More from Series Magritte* (2009)
Ed Baker's *Goodnight (2009)*
David Huntsperger's Postindustrial *Folktales* (2010)
Gautam Verma's *The Opacity of Frosted Glass* (2011)
rob mclennan's *Kate Street* (2011)
Garin Cycholl's *The Bonegatherer* (2011)
j/j hastain's *autobiography of my gender* (2011)
Kristina Marie Darling's *narrative (dis)continuities: prose experiments by younger american writers* (2013)
Jay Besemer's *A New Territory Sought* (2013)
Joel Chace's *One Web* (2014)
Garin Cycholl's *Horse Country* (2014)
Eileen Tabios' *I Forgot Light Burns* (2015)
lars palm's *look who's singing* (2015)
Ed Baker's *Neighbor* (2015)
Tom Beckett's *Appearances: A Novel in Fragments* (2015) Charles Perrone's Out of Alphabetical Order (2015)
Piotr Gwiazda's *Aspects of Strangers* (2015)
Freke Räihä's a *[title missing] – quality of motion* (2016)
Kristian Carlsson's *A Crack at the Origins* (2016)
Matina L. Stamatakis' *A Late Sketch of Final Doves* (2017)
Mark Young's *The Perfume of the Abyss* (2019)

Lopez's, Bloomberg-Rissman's, and *Marshall's The End of
   the World Project, vol 1 and vol 2* (2019)
Joel Chace's *Threnodies* (2019)
López's and Mukherjee's *Conversation about Withering* (2020)
George J. Farrah's *Swans through the House* (2020)
Minton's, Magallón's, and Crouch's *Letters* (2022)
Serena Piccoli's *gulp/gasp* (2022)

The books/e-books can be found at www.moriapoetry.com.

www.ingramcontent.com/pod-product-compliance
Lightning Source LLC
Chambersburg PA
CBHW051349040426
42453CB00007B/486